CONTENTS

INTRODUCTION

Welcome to the fast and furious world of skateboarding. Many people will, at one time or another, come into contact with a skateboard, whether it's a cheap supermarket version or a high-end professional set-up. What most people don't get to see is the vast network of skatepark terrain, skateboard tricks, 'skatespeak' and colourful characters.

We are going to open up that world and invite you to learn some basic tricks and some high-end tricks that should keep you going throughout your skateboarding life.

SKATESPEAK

Throughout this book you will come across some language that you may not be familiar with. Here is a guide to help you.

Coping - *The metal edge running along the top of a ramp or block.*
Fakie - *Riding backwards.*
Goofy - *Skaters who skate with the right foot forward, at the front of the deck.*
Grind - *When the trucks (metal wheel mounts) grind along coping or metal.*
Regular - *Skaters who skate with the left foot forward, at the front of the deck.*
Shred - *To skate fast and confidently.*

GUIDE TO ARROWS

Throughout the book we have used red arrows like this ➡ to indicate the action of the body and direction the skateboard is travelling.

EQUIPMENT

Before you start skateboarding you need a skateboard set-up. A set-up consists of a deck, a pair of trucks and a set of wheels. There are lots of other smaller parts on a skateboard. Make sure that you know all of their names and the jobs that they do.

SKATEBOARD DECK

A typical skateboard deck is made from 7 plies (layers) of Canadian maple wood glued and pressed together. This process ensures that the deck is strong but flexible.

GRIPTAPE

Griptape is a sandpaper type material that is applied to the top sheet of the deck to keep you steady and positioned. Griptape also helps when flipping the board with your feet. Griptape is self-adhesive and should be applied before adding the trucks and wheels.

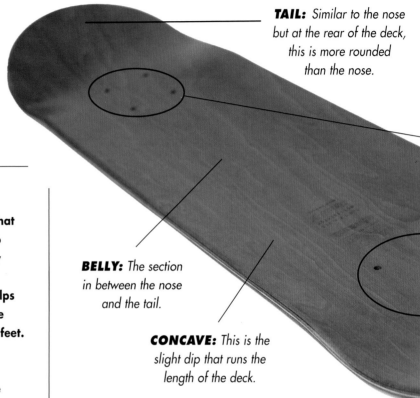

TAIL: Similar to the nose but at the rear of the deck, this is more rounded than the nose.

BELLY: The section in between the nose and the tail.

CONCAVE: This is the slight dip that runs the length of the deck.

TRUCKS

The trucks are where the science comes in. Your trucks control how loose or how tight your ride will be. By turning the nut on the kingpin you can adjust each truck until you feel comfortable with the way the skateboard turns and carves.

AXLE: The steel rod that you bolt your wheels onto. This rod is embedded into the hanger.

KINGPIN: The bolt that holds the hanger onto the baseplate.

BUSHINGS: Two rubber doughnuts that sit on the kingpin and control the steering.

HANGER: The main alloy body of the truck (used for grinding tricks).

BASEPLATE: The section that bolts onto the deck and houses the hanger.

NUTS AND BOLTS

A set of eight nuts and bolts hold the trucks to the griptaped deck. Most skateboarding bolts come with an Allen key included in the package.

WHEELS

All skateboard wheels are made from a hard plastic called urethane. Usually they are white but some coloured wheels are available. Each wheel takes two bearings, one in each side.

BOLT HOLES: Four holes at the front and four at the back used to attach the trucks.

NOSE: The rounded front end of the deck which lifts up slightly. This is a bit more pointy than the tail.

BEARINGS

Bearings come in sets of eight (two per wheel). The speed and quality is measured in an ABEC rating. Basic bearings will be around ABEC 3, and the better quality speed bearings will be ABEC 7. Top of the range bearings are ceramic and are very expensive.

SKATETOOL

A skatetool can tighten or loosen your wheel nuts, stiffen or loosen your trucks' turning ability, and hold the nuts when bolting the trucks to the deck. You should always have a skatetool in your bag or pocket when out skateboarding in case you need to make adjustments.

KNOW YOUR TERRAIN

The term skateboarding terrain can be applied to anything — from your back garden to a huge ramp in a world-class skatepark. The list is endless but some good terrain can be easily found at your local skatepark. Before you turn up board-in-hand and ready to 'shred', let's go through what you should expect to come across in your new arena.

Indoor skatepark

TRANSITIONS

Almost all skateparks will have some form of transition.

A transition is any form made from wood that has a bend or curve in it. Quarterpipes have one transition (bend) and can range from 60 centimetres high right up to 10 metres high. Mini-ramps and vert ramps have two transitions facing each other. This allows you to flow from one transition to another without stopping. Transitions can be tight or mellow depending on the steepness of the curve: the steeper the curve the tighter the transition. Tight transitions are harder to skate. There will be many transitions of varying steepness in any one skatepark. Make sure you start on the mellow ones!

HANDRAILS

Handrails are where the more confident skateboarders will spend most of their time.

Made from steel and ranging in size and steepness, handrails will either be set into the centre of a set of stairs or sometimes down the centre of a flatbank. Handrails should not be approached until you have the confidence and skill to skate them. Learn to skate a flatbar first and then gradually move onto handrails.

Handrail

Flatbank

Transition

TOP TIP

Never skate handrails or vert ramps by yourself! Always session these obstacles with a bunch of friends so that, in the unlikely event that you injure yourself, there will be help close at hand. Always wear pads when you are trying to master handrails or vert ramps.

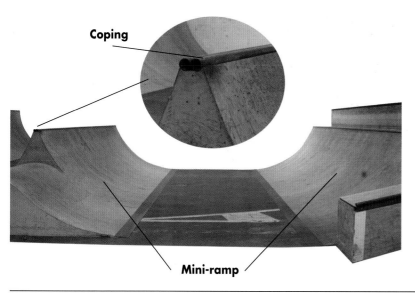

Coping

Mini-ramp

Mini-ramps are great fun. They come in all kinds of sizes, most often they are around 1.5–1.8 metres high and 6 metres wide.

They have mid-range transitions at either side and have platforms at both ends to stand on and drop in from. The aim is to start at one side, drop in and carve, grind and slide for as long as you can. Running along the top edge of each transition is a long length of steel tubing called the coping. This is what you grind and slide on.

The vert ramp is the big daddy of the mini-ramp.
These can also differ in size, but the transition will always lead to a 30-60 cm vertical section at the very top of the ramp. The ramps are so big that when you drop in one side you go so fast that you will catch air on the other side, flying out and hopefully landing back into the ramps and so on. This takes a long time to perfect and pads and helmet must be worn at all times. Start by doing big long carves from the bottom and working your way up. Always take it one step at a time.

Vert ramp   Vertical section

Scattered around the skatepark will be blocks of various sizes. Some will be placed on the floor and some may run down the sides of flatbanks.

Blocks are great for learning how to slide and grind. As with all skatepark obstacles, start on the smaller versions and work your way up. You will need to learn the ollie in order to jump onto the blocks to achieve a grind or a slide.

You will also find steel flatbars in most parks. Flatbars are lengths of freestanding steel coping that are great for learning how to balance and distribute your weight. Flatbars are harder to skate because of the freestanding element. Learn boardslides and grind on blocks first then take them to the flatbar.

Block   Flatbar

WARMING UP & PADDING UP

*L*ike all high-energy sports, skateboarding requires that you get your muscles warmed up and ready to 'get gnarly' for an entire session. Even after you've followed these simple stretches you should start your session by just doing some simple flatland manoeuvres before hitting the ramps and blocks.

Sit down with both legs together.
Support one leg with your hand and slowly slide the foot of the other leg up to your knee. Repeat this with the other leg. This will get you ready for the next few stretches.

Maintain the same position as the first stretch.
Place the opposite hand on the inside of the bent knee. At the same time swing the other arm behind you so that it lines up with the straight leg. Push down on the knee and swing your shoulders and hips around so that you stretch your back muscles. Repeat on the other side.

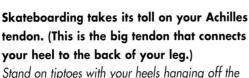

After you've stretched your knee ligaments a few times go for this tried and tested classic: touching your toes.
Sit down and keep your legs flat against the floor. Keep your back as straight as you can and touch both sets of toes with both hands. This will stretch your shoulder muscles, back and arms, which is ideal for when you are reaching for your deck during a grab trick.

Skateboarding takes its toll on your Achilles tendon. (This is the big tendon that connects your heel to the back of your leg.)
Stand on tiptoes with your heels hanging off the edge of a small quarterpipe (so that your heels are in mid-air). Keeping your feet as solid as possible, slowly lean forward so that you can feel the back of your heel and tendon gently stretching. Do this for around a minute.

Last, but not least, is a simple knee stretch.
Stand upright and lift your leg and foot up behind you so that you are standing on one leg. Grab your foot and gently pull and stretch your knee muscles. Repeat with the other leg.

TOP TIP
Have a quick jog on the spot and shake down with your arms to get the blood flowing.

Most skateboard parks demand that you wear pads and a helmet if you wish to skate at their facility. This is a good thing to do, especially if you are still learning, as elbows and knees are often the first body parts to come into contact with the floor if you take a slam. All good skateparks will have a set of pads that you can either borrow or hire. So get padded up!

HELMET

The skateboard helmet is made from a tough plastic compound and is lined with a comfortable foam layer.

You can get custom helmets with your favourite skateboard company's logo embossed or printed on. There are thousands of different designs so it's easy to grab yourself a unique skid lid!

Knee pad

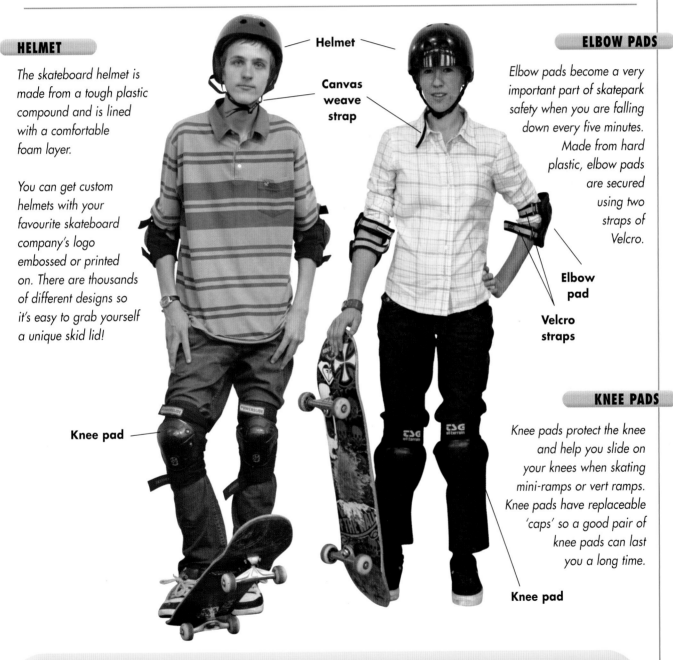

Helmet

Canvas
weave
strap

ELBOW PADS

Elbow pads become a very important part of skatepark safety when you are falling down every five minutes. Made from hard plastic, elbow pads are secured using two straps of Velcro.

**Elbow
pad**

**Velcro
straps**

KNEE PADS

Knee pads protect the knee and help you slide on your knees when skating mini-ramps or vert ramps. Knee pads have replaceable 'caps' so a good pair of knee pads can last you a long time.

Knee pad

TOP TIP
When skating mini- or vert ramps it's good to learn how to knee slide.
Practise falling to your knees on the transition and sliding down the curve on
the plastic caps with both legs together.

PUSHING OFF

Now that you are warmed up and ready to rock you can get moving on all four wheels. This is called 'pushing off'. The more confident that you become with pushing off the quicker and more fluid you will become at it. Before we get into the technicalities of a good push let's see if you are goofy or regular footed...

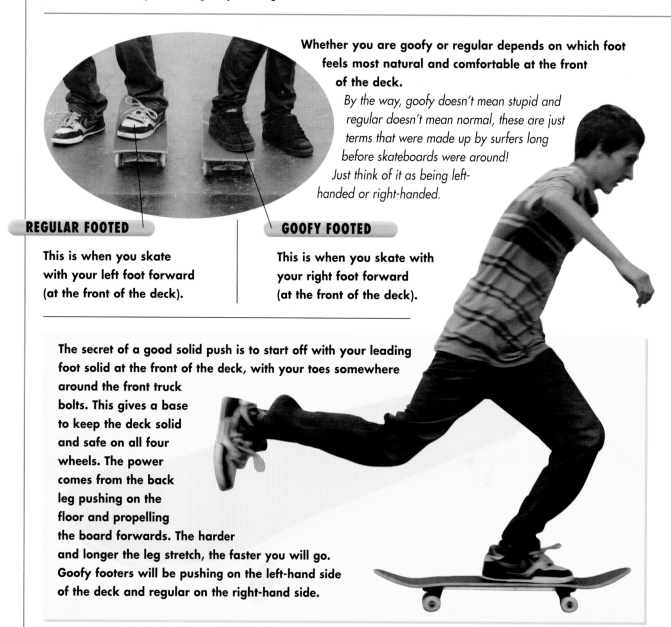

Whether you are goofy or regular depends on which foot feels most natural and comfortable at the front of the deck.

By the way, goofy doesn't mean stupid and regular doesn't mean normal, these are just terms that were made up by surfers long before skateboards were around! Just think of it as being left-handed or right-handed.

REGULAR FOOTED

This is when you skate with your left foot forward (at the front of the deck).

GOOFY FOOTED

This is when you skate with your right foot forward (at the front of the deck).

The secret of a good solid push is to start off with your leading foot solid at the front of the deck, with your toes somewhere around the front truck bolts. This gives a base to keep the deck solid and safe on all four wheels. The power comes from the back leg pushing on the floor and propelling the board forwards. The harder and longer the leg stretch, the faster you will go. Goofy footers will be pushing on the left-hand side of the deck and regular on the right-hand side.

TOP TIP
Find a smooth floor surface. Run and slide in your socks and see which foot is in front. This is the foot you should use at the front of your skateboard.

Once you have pushed away with a few solid strokes you will need to plant your pushing foot back onto the deck.

Try to get your back foot onto the griptape and over the rear bolts. (You can see the bolt heads on top of your griptape.) When you are stable and rolling confidently you will need to slowly re-adjust your front foot from the pointing forward position to pointing sideways; this way it locks your stance into the safest and most comfortable position. When your feet are both horizontal across the deck you are ready to try some carving, turning and tricks.

STEP 1

Starting off from a standstill, place your leading foot at the front of the deck and rest your pushing foot at the toe side of the stationary skateboard (around the back wheel seems to be the best and most comfortable).

You should keep your balance and body weight over the centre of the skateboard.

STEP 2

With your front foot solid on the deck slowly start to move the board forward with your pushing leg.

As you move forward your foot will naturally start to go towards being on its tiptoes.

STEP 3

As your pushing leg reaches the end of one solid push you will need to lift it off the ground, keeping your position and balance over the centre of the skateboard. Start to return the pushing leg to the deck.

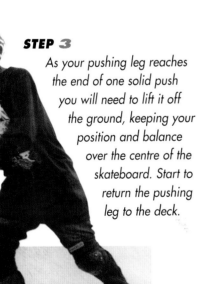

STEP 4

With your pushing leg now returning to the back of the deck you will be freewheeling forwards. In order to keep this a good stable ride your back foot should now be on the griptape and heading towards covering the rear truck bolts.

MOVING, TURNING & CARVING

You are now mobile! Once you've found your balance and are happy with getting yourself moving forward at a manageable speed you are going to want to explore turning, carving and some of the tricks that come with being a skateboarder. The easiest and most important part of this process is turning the board while riding on it forward.

FOOT POSITION

This picture shows what your stance should be like while you are moving forward.
Your feet should be positioned over both sets of truck bolts and central across the deck, with a slight overhang from both your heels and your toes.

HEELSIDE PRESSURE

Whilst moving forwards apply pressure to the heelside of the skateboard.
As you apply pressure, slowly but surely you will start to turn away from the straight line that you have been maintaining. This heel-based turn is called a frontside carve because you will be turning with your chest facing out to the front side. The more pressure that you apply the faster and tighter this turn will be.

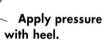

Apply pressure with heel.

TOESIDE PRESSURE

Whilst moving forwards start to put pressure on the toeside of the deck.
As this pressure mounts you will start to turn backside. The pressure that you put on the deck with your toes will take your carve backside and you will be turning with your back facing out to the front side.

Apply pressure with toes.

FRONTSIDE CARVE

STEP 1

Reach a manageable speed and start to apply pressure to the heel side of the deck, moving your arms to keep your body balanced.

STEP 2

The skateboard should turn to the side, away from the straight line that you were on. Keep the heel pressure applied and follow the carve with your body and balance.

STEP 3

As you reach the end of the turn or carve release the pressure and you will start to straighten out again. You can do these turns as slowly or as quickly as you want.

BACKSIDE CARVE

STEP 1

Reach a comfortable speed and put pressure on the deck with both sets of toes. You will feel the skateboard starting to turn. To help you stay balanced over the board, hold out your arms if you need to.

STEP 2

The pressure from your toes should have you carving backside (your back will be slowly facing forwards as you take in the carve).

STEP 3

At the end of the carve, or turn, release the pressure from your toes and you will straighten out again. (These turns are great for carving around a long bend.)

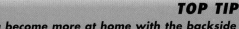

TOP TIP

As you become more at home with the backside and frontside carves you will be able to change from one to another creating a snake effect. Push away with two solid pushes and then do as many backside to frontside carves as you can and repeat.

THE OLLIE

*A*fter learning how to get moving, turning and carving, the ollie is THE most important trick you will ever learn on a skateboard. It is pretty much the basis for all other tricks. You will need this trick to get into and out of most of the things you will want to learn.

THE OLLIE

The ollie is the skateboard jump. When you've learnt this trick you will be able to get up onto things and jump over things, so as you would expect it's an important piece of the skateboard puzzle.

STEP 1

Put your front foot just behind the four front truck bolts. Take up the correct foot position for the ollie. Crouch down slightly with your knees bent.

Bend knees

Your back foot should be at the very back of the deck with your toes in the middle of the tail.

Put your front foot just behind the four front truck bolts.

Correct foot positioning for the ollie.

STEP 2

Kick down on the tail with your back foot as hard as you can, this will produce the 'POP' as it hits the floor. When you kick down with the back leg, release the pressure from your front leg and let the board's nose point upwards.

STEP 3

Now you need to jump, but at the same time scrape the side of your front foot up the griptape and release the pressure from your back foot. The slide of the foot will drag the board into the air and the release of the back leg will allow the deck to jump up.

Slide front foot up griptape.

Release pressure from back foot.

STEP 4

Keep your balance over the deck and travel with the skateboard back to the ground. As you hit the ground with all four wheels at the same time, compress a little and stay balanced. You've just done an ollie! Well done.

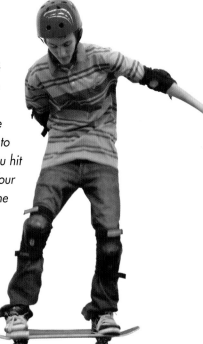

THE OLLIE WHILE MOVING

STEP 1

Push to start and while keeping your body weight over the deck, start to crouch down slightly.

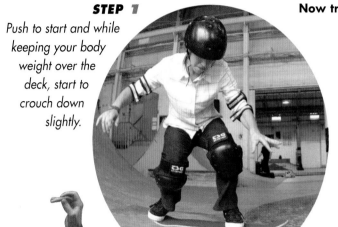

Now try the ollie while moving forwards. This will help with the fluid motion you need to pop a really good ollie.

STEP 2

As your speed levels out get ready to push the tail to the ground with your back foot.

STEP 3

Kick down on the tail and let the pressure off the front foot. This allows the nose of the deck to point upwards. Then drag your front foot sideways up the griptape and release the pressure from your back leg. Your board should level out in the air.

STEP 4

Bring your board back to the ground, keeping your balance over the deck. You should now be level over the skateboard and riding away with a big grin on your face. The trick to learning the ollie is never give up, it takes a while but once you have it you'll have it forever. Enjoy!

When you hit the ground bend your knees slightly.

HOW TO FLIP THE BOARD

Most people think of the board flipping when you mention skateboarding to them. This is a tricky process and takes a lot of practice to perfect. Flipping the board is something you are going to want to do as soon as you step on a board but you must learn the ollie first. The kickflip is probably the first flip trick you will learn so follow the steps and get flipping...

HOW TO FLIP THE BOARD

You need to do an ollie before you perform the kicking part of this trick. The back foot is still in the ollie position (toes in the centre of the tail), but the front foot is slightly off towards the heel edge of the deck.

Front foot

Back foot

Correct foot positions for a flip.

STEP 1

When you are moving at a medium speed, hit down on the tail with some force, jump and start to scrape your front foot up the griptape.

STEP 2

As you scrape your front foot up the tape, start to scrape towards the heel edge of the deck (in an ollie you would just scrape forwards). This motion will start the deck turning. Remember to stay central over the deck at all times.

TOP TIP
Try learning this trick standing still or even on a carpeted surface (some people also practise on a deck with no wheels or trucks!!!). It's all about the technique with the kickflip, you need to get a good flick after the ollie.

STEP 3

This is called the flick. As your front foot comes to the end of the scrape and off the deck it will produce a flick. (If you've done the scrape quickly enough.)

Now the deck is in full motion and should be turning underneath your body and feet.

STEP 4

Watch the board turn underneath you. As the deck turns a full 360° along its length the griptape side of the board will become visible.

As you see the tape you need to get both of your feet ready to cover the truck bolts for touch down.

STEP 5

As your feet 'catch' the skateboard get ready to ride away at the same speed you began with. As with all skateboard tricks this is about trial and error and practise is the key. This trick is a must for your trick bag.

TOP TIP
Always stay with the board as it goes through the kickflip motion, keeping your shoulders above your feet throughout the trick.

HOW TO MAKE IT GRIND

*T*he other thing that you will be itching to do once you have the ollie perfected is to 'grind'. The easiest grind to do first is the 50-50 grind. This is where both trucks are grinding along at the same time. The 50-50 can be done on ledges, handrails, at the top of ramps and on blocks.

MAKE IT GRIND

To perform a 50-50 grind you need to do a nice clean ollie slightly higher than the edge/rail that you want to grind. You need to go slightly faster than usual because you will feel some resistance as you land on the edge that you want to grind.

STEP 1

As you approach the block hit the tail and start your ollie about 30 cm before the obstacle starts. You are aiming to get both of your trucks up onto the lip of the obstacle.

STEP 2

After you've popped a high enough ollie to get onto the block, level out the deck and trucks over the grinding edge. Aim the trucks to land central on the grinding surface. Your body weight needs to be central over the entire skateboard.

Stand over the truck bolts and travel along while keeping your body weight over the moving skateboard.

STEP 3

As you land you will feel some resistance, this is the metal of the trucks hitting the metal of the grinding edge. The speed that you are travelling will determine the speed at which you grind. If you stop dead you will need to go faster or lean back slightly as if to push into the grind.

STEP 4

As you reach the end of your grind you are going to want to lift the front of the deck upwards slightly to help you drop off the edge. Apply some weight to the tail and lift up the nose. This is so that when you come off the grind you will hit the floor with all four wheels rather than dipping down or falling backwards.

STEP 5

As you come off the grind make sure that all four wheels are in contact with the floor and you are moving fast enough to ride away smoothly.

Correct position of trucks when grinding.

TOP TIP

Never try to grind an edge that hasn't been waxed first. When you know what you want to grind, apply a thin layer of skate wax. This reduces the resistance that you feel and will help you on your travels. You can also apply wax directly to the trucks.

SLIDING A FLATBAR

The 50-50 introduces an element of balance to your skateboard experience and we are now going to look at the ultimate balance trick — the boardslide on a freestanding flatbar. This trick is performed down handrails and is often the first trick that a professional will do to test out a handrail that goes down stairs.

SLIDING A FLATBAR

STEP 1

This is called a backside boardslide. Roll towards the bar with your heels and back facing towards the bar. You will slide quite fast with this trick so build up to the speed you need with practise slides.

STEP 2

You will be using the ollie technique but using it to land sideways onto the bar (see frontside ollie). You need half a frontside ollie to get onto the bar.

Pop the tail on the floor and start your ollie.

STEP 3

As you ollie onto the bar throw your shoulders around slightly so that the momentum takes you onto the bar.

STEP 4

Get ready to balance as the board stabilises centrally on the bar. You will start to slide along. By now you will be facing the front and sliding forwards.

It's very important to keep the deck level and your weight distributed across the board.

STEP 5

Hold the boardslide pose until the end of the bar and get ready to help the skateboard come off forwards (rather than plopping off sideways and coming to a standstill).

STEP 6

At the end of the boardslide start turning the deck back to the riding away position. Don't do this until you know the board will come off the bar clean.

Use your front leg to push the front of the deck away from the bar.

STEP 7

The skateboard should now be clear of the bar and you can continue to slide the deck around until you are riding away the same way that you were before you ollied onto the bar. Nice one!

TOP TIP

When you are in mid-boardslide pose your chest should be facing the way that you are sliding, and you need to use your arms to keep you level on the bar. Imagine that you are walking on a tightrope.

DROPPING IN ON A RAMP

*U*ntil now we have just looked at moving around on flat ground where it's easy to control your speed and direction. Now, we're going to look at transitions.

TRANSITIONS

A transition is a bend or curve in a ramp, so a big vert ramp has two transitions, one at each side. Basically anything with a curve in can be called a transition. It's easier to practise dropping in on a quarterpipe first. These have only one transition and lead out onto the flat ground rather than going straight into another transition.

DROPPING IN

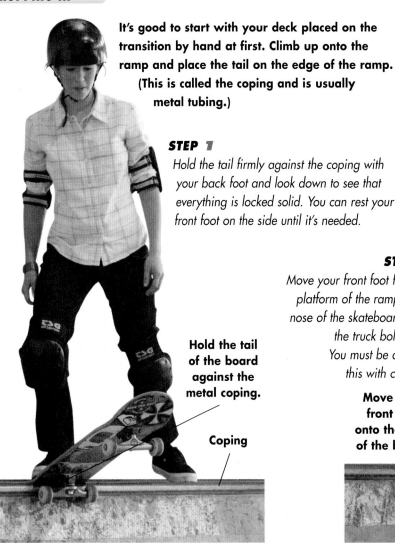

It's good to start with your deck placed on the transition by hand at first. Climb up onto the ramp and place the tail on the edge of the ramp. (This is called the coping and is usually metal tubing.)

STEP 1

Hold the tail firmly against the coping with your back foot and look down to see that everything is locked solid. You can rest your front foot on the side until it's needed.

STEP 2

Move your front foot from the platform of the ramp onto the nose of the skateboard (across the truck bolts again). You must be able to do this with confidence!

Move your front foot onto the nose of the board.

Hold the tail of the board against the metal coping.

Coping

The key to dropping in well and safely is confidence. Make sure you are padded up when you are trying this trick and you will be fine.

STEP 3

When you have both feet on the deck start to lean forwards keeping your feet on the griptape at all times. You will be moving very fast and need to stay with the board at all times.

Hold your arms out to steady yourself.

Bend your knees.

STEP 4

As you start to move into the transition and away from the coping lean forward and get ready for the speed of the ride. Push down on your front wheels as soon as you drop away from the coping, so that all four wheels are down as early as possible. Stay with the skateboard as it rides down the ramp.

TOP TIP
Stamp the board down so that it follows the transition of the ramp and doesn't do a wheelie all the way to the floor.

ROCK & ROLL

This trick demands that you ride up the transition rather than go down it as with the drop in. The 'Rock & Roll' is an old traditional trick often used when skating a ramp. The idea is that you drop in on one side and then do a rock & roll on the other side. Now you have learnt how to drop in, maybe it's time for some rock and roll....!

ROCK & ROLL

STEP 1

Ride towards the transition with the speed that you will need to reach the metal coping. Keep both your feet stable over the truck bolts. Bend your knees slightly in order to feel relaxed as you hit the ramp.

Bend knees

Coping

STEP 2

Keeping the same body position and stance, start to ride up the transition and get ready to come into contact with the coping at the top of the ramp. Look at the coping and start to visualise the centre/belly of your skateboard coming into contact with it.

STEP 3

Now at the top of the ramp you need to lift the front wheels slightly as you go past the coping, but don't go too far. Stay with the board as it reaches the top.

STEP 4

As the centre of your skateboard reaches the coping, push down with your front foot and make contact between the belly of your board and the metal coping.

Belly of the board makes contact with the coping.

STEP 5

As soon as you feel the contact between wood and metal it's time to start the turn back towards where you came from.

STEP 6

With the 'Rock' completed it's time for the 'Roll'. As you come away from the top of the ramp put pressure on the tail and swing the nose back around away from the ramp.

Lift the nose by putting pressure on the tail.

STEP 7

The turn for the rock & roll is all in the shoulders. Swing your arms around to help turn the board.

Swing the board around on the back wheels.

STEP 8

Put the front wheels down so that you are riding on all four. This is a quick trick and is probably best done in sections whilst learning. Dropping in and riding up and down transitions will help build up your confidence.

ROCK FAKIE

The rock fakie is the dangerous brother of the rock & roll. This trick involves riding up the transition and lapping over the coping/edge and then coming back in fakie (backwards). As you can imagine, it's easy to get stuck on the coping, and yet again it's confidence that will help you master this trick.

HOW TO ROCK FAKIE

As with a lot of transition tricks you need to keep your feet solid over the truck bolts and try not to shuffle about on the deck too much.

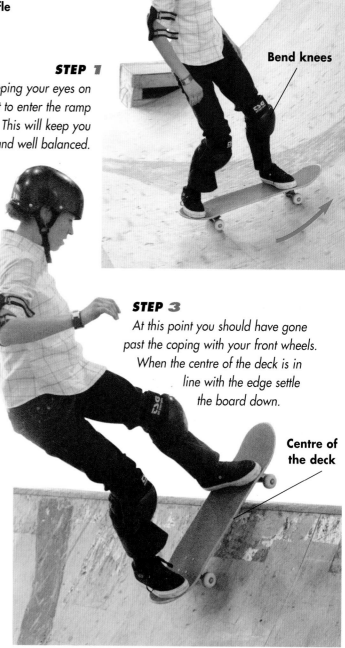

Top edge

Bend knees

STEP 1

Approach the transition, keeping your eyes on the top edge. As you start to enter the ramp bend your knees slightly. This will keep you relaxed and well balanced.

STEP 2

As you get near the coping, get ready to press down on the tail with the back foot to lift the nose so that you lap over the coping.

Pressing down on the tail will lift the nose.

STEP 3

At this point you should have gone past the coping with your front wheels. When the centre of the deck is in line with the edge settle the board down.

Centre of the deck

STEP 4

Now your board should be balanced like a boardslide on the edge of the coping.

STEP 5

Now you need to go back down the transition fakie.

Gravity will take you back down the ramp. Lift the front wheels again to unlock you from the coping.

STEP 6

This will happen quickly so be prepared! Keep your body and balance central over the entire skateboard as you ride the transition.

STEP 7

Wipe the sweat from your brow and ride away fakie.

BACKSIDE 50-50 AXLE STALLS

By now you should have dropping in, rock & rolls and rock fakies sorted. The next logical progression is to get your trucks on the metal coping of the ramp. When you've learnt the 50-50 axle stall you will be able to string together all these tricks and skate a mini-ramp with ease.

THE 50-50 AXLE STALL

STEP 1

Ride up towards the coping with enough speed to reach it. This time you are going to need to get the whole deck up on the top of the ramp.

Coping

STEP 2

As you get to the coping lift your front wheels slightly to let them pass the metal edge. You are aiming to lap your back truck onto the coping.

Lift front wheels.

Press down on the tail to lift front wheels.

STEP 3

As you feel the back truck come into contact with the coping, turn the deck using your legs and shoulders so that the nose swings around and becomes parallel with the coping.

TOP TIP

The 50-50 axle stall is a blind trick as you can't see your trucks as they come into contact with the coping. You need to practise until you learn how to feel the trick with your feet. As your trucks lap over the coping you will feel a slight thud, this is when you know it's safe to put the front down as well.

STEP 4

When the front trucks are over the coping set them down. You should now be standing over the skateboard with both trucks firmly on the coping.

Correct position for trucks.

STEP 5

Time to escape! As soon as you are sure that you are on both trucks lift the front truck again and get ready to turn back into the transition.

STEP 6

Swing the front of the deck back into the transition and treat the next stage as dropping in (see pages 22-23), but from the truck rather than the tail.

STEP 7

Momentum will do the rest and you should be riding away. Trust the skateboard at this point and stay with it.

FRONTSIDE & BACKSIDE OLLIE

There are hundreds of tricks that can be done on a skateboard. After you've learnt the basics you can start stringing tricks together and even making up your own. In this next section we are going to look at some of the more complex tricks that will give you ideas and help you become king or queen of the skatepark!

FRONTSIDE 180 OLLIE

The frontside 180 ollie is where your chest is thrown forward to turn you 180°.

STEP 1
As the name suggests, this is an ollie turning 180°. First get your feet in a normal ollie position and crouch down.

STEP 2
Hit the tail, swinging your arms for extra momentum.

STEP 3
As you do the ollie scrape, throw your body around 90° and take your board with it.

STEP 4
By this time you should have moved the deck around 180° in the air.

STEP 5
When the skateboard has turned a full 180° put the front wheels down first. Then settle the back wheels down and ride away fakie.

The backside ollie is where your back is thrown round to turn you 180°.

STEP 1

This is the opposite of the frontside ollie. You will be throwing your body around towards your back this time. Get your feet in the ollie position. Get ready to pop.

STEP 3

Once you are in the air throw your body and board around turning through 90°.

STEP 2

Hit the tail, scrape up an ollie and swing your arms and hips into a backside movement.

STEP 4

You can land this trick 90° on the floor but you will need to slide the other 90°.

STEP 5

As you touch down slide the board around until you are riding away fakie.

FRONTSIDE & BACKSIDE FLIPS

We are going to start mixing tricks now. The frontside flip is a frontside ollie and a kickflip combined. The same goes for the backside flip. Both are crowd pleasers and can be done down stairs or across gaps. They're great to do after you've frontside or backside ollied something. Add a flip and impress your mates.

THE FRONTSIDE FLIP

STEP 1

The motion of this trick is exactly the same as a frontside 180 ollie but hang your front foot slightly off the heel edge as with the kickflip.

STEP 2

Scrape and kick out to the side. Start to ollie whilst getting ready to flick at the same time.

STEP 3

At the mid-point of the frontside kickflip you should have frontside ollied the board and kicked out to the side.

STEP 4

The board flips and turns 180°. You need to stay above it at all times. When the board is four wheels down ride away fakie.

THE BACKSIDE FLIP

STEP 1
You are going to throw this flip around 180° with your back facing forwards. As you prepare to hit the tail start your body swinging in a backside direction.

STEP 2
Pop the tail and start to ollie backside. At the same time get ready to kick out and to the side.

STEP 3
After the ollie and the kick the board should have started flipping.

STEP 4
Keeping the deck under you as you go, get ready to take it to the floor.

STEP 5
Land with all four wheels down and ride away fakie.

THE POP SHOVE-IT & 360 KICKFLIP

Both of these tricks involve the board turning around underneath you. The 360 kickflip is the most tricky as it turns 360° as well as flipping! The pop shove-it is a lot easier but you need to learn this in order to do a 360 kickflip.

THE POP SHOVE-IT

This trick is good for getting used to moving the board around under your feet.

Hit the tail and scoop it around at the same time.

STEP 1
Start an ollie but instead of just hitting the tail, scoop it around at the same time. This will start the board turning around. This trick is all in the back foot.

STEP 2
Don't scrape so much with the front foot. Just pop and scoop it around 180° with the back foot.

STEP 3
As it comes around 180°, stay over the deck and stamp it down. Your board will now be backwards under your feet.

STEP 4
Both feet should now be over the truck bolts ready for a clean ride away.

THE 360 KICKFLIP

With the 360 flip we are going to push the deck around 360° as well as kickflipping it. At the same time we need to use an ollie to get the board in the air.

STEP 1

For this trick you need your front foot in a kickflip position hanging over the heel edge of the deck. Your back foot is at the corner of the tail (toe edge).

Hit down and push the board around with the back foot.

Use the front foot to flip the board.

STEP 2

Start with an ollie procedure then start to push the board around with your back foot. At the same time start to kick out to the side as with a standard kickflip.

STEP 3

Shove hard with the back foot to turn around 360°. The board should be flipping because you've kicked as well.

STEP 4

Stay above this flipping, turning deck and when you've spun it 360° get ready to stamp it down.

STEP 5

When you've 360 flipped the deck, land your feet over the truck bolts in order to stay stable. Well done, you've nailed a 360 kickflip – one of the hardest tricks in the book!

FRONTSIDE BOARDSLIDE & K-GRIND

The frontside boardslide is the harder brother of the regular boardslide (page 20-21) and the K-Grind (krooked grind) is a cool trick using the front truck to grind along. Both are used by professional skateboarders, often down handrails, but don't worry as they are easy to learn on smaller skatepark obstacles.

(page 20-21)

FRONTSIDE BOARDSLIDE

STEP 1
With your chest facing the flatbar, ollie high enough to get above it. Keep your eyes on the flatbar as well.

STEP 2
As you ollie direct the deck towards the flatbar, you need to get the belly of the board right on top.

STEP 3
Land with the centre of the deck on the flatbar and twist your body to balance over it.

STEP 4
As you slide along be aware that the end of the bar will be coming and prepare to turn off and ride away forwards.

STEP 5
As you drop off the flatbar use your front foot to direct the board so that you ride away straight.

TOP TIP
Keep your body twisted to help stay balanced throughout the slide.

STEP 1

Ride along the side of the block as close as you can with your back facing it.

STEP 2

Pop your ollie and use your front foot to direct the skateboard. Jab the nose and front truck onto the edge of the block.

STEP 3

When you have made contact with the front truck take the weight off your back leg. This allows the back of the skateboard to rise.

STEP 4

As you reach the end of the block push forwards with your front foot and level the back of the skateboard out so that you are horizontal.

Correct truck position during the K-Grind.

STEP 5

Land on all four wheels and straighten out riding away the same way that you began.

Toeside wheel running freely.

The heel side of the board crushed against the inside wheel.

TOP TIP

**Keep your weight forward and over the nose whilst doing a K-Grind.
Use your arms to keep you balanced.**

SLIDE 180 & THE FAKIE KICKFLIP

There are a few different ways to ride fakie. When you do a 180 ollie frontside or backside you will end up riding backwards. Sliding around is a quicker, easier option. You can do this move and keep your speed, ideal for learning fakie tricks, such as the fakie kickflip (a kickflip whilst travelling backwards).

SLIDE 180

STEP 1

Ride along forwards with your front foot over the nose and your back foot over the tail.

STEP 2

When you are ready to start sliding around give your shoulders a big swing as if you were going to spin around on the spot.

STEP 3

With the momentum you have built up, use your back foot to start pushing the rear of the deck around.

STEP 4

Keep pushing the back of the deck around whilst pivoting on the front wheels. Lift the rear wheels slightly if you are sticking.

STEP 5

As you reach the 180° that you are sliding, start to stop the push and get ready to ride away fakie.

STEP 1

As this trick suggests it's a kickflip riding backwards (fakie). Start off riding fakie, maybe slide around so that you are travelling backwards.

STEP 2

Get your feet in the kickflip position (see pages 16-17), pop the ollie and get ready to flick out to the side.

STEP 3

Stay over the board as it spins.

STEP 4

As the board comes around to the griptape side place your feet back onto the deck.

STEP 5

Land with your feet over the truckbolts and ride away fakie.

TOP TIP

**Always look down at what you are doing when trying the fakie kickflip.
This trick becomes easier the more that you ride around backwards.**

PUMPING A VERT RAMP

*I*n most big skateparks you will find a vert ramp. It is often placed in the corner looking huge and scary. It takes a while to become good at skating vert but it can be great fun and as close to flying like a bird as you will probably ever get. Before you attempt to drop in or catch some air it's a good idea to have a pump around. This means taking big sweeps of the ramp from side to side or up and down, forwards and fakie.*

PUMPING UP THE RAMP

STEP 1

Start this move on the flat section of the vert ramp and do a few pushes so you are travelling towards the transition.

Bend your knees.

STEP 2

When you reach the middle of the transition, start to bend your legs and compress into the ramp. Your arms should have swung forwards to propel you upwards.

STEP 3

Keeping your legs bent, get as high past the transition as you can while being comfortable.

STEP 4

As you slow down you will start to come down the ramp fakie.

Start to straighten your legs.

STEP 5

When you have passed the transition straighten out fully. You've just pumped! Phew…

A BIG BACKSIDE CARVE

STEP 1

Ride towards the vert ramp's transition. At the bottom, start to lean in with your chest but keep your speed.

STEP 2

As you ride higher into the transition, lean into the ramp with your chest more.

STEP 3

This leaning will push you around so that you are horizontal with the flat bottom. When you have reached the highest point, turn into the ramp and point the board back towards the flat bottom.

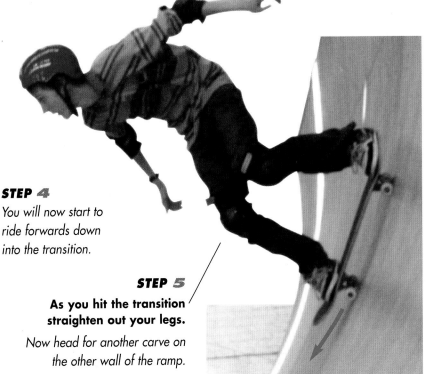

STEP 4

You will now start to ride forwards down into the transition.

STEP 5

As you hit the transition straighten out your legs.

Now head for another carve on the other wall of the ramp.

TOP TIP
Try doing smaller tighter carves as well as big long mellow ones.
They feel amazing!

SKATEPARK DIET

Skateboarding takes loads of energy so you need to have a healthy, balanced diet to keep you doing tricks all day! A lot of indoor skateparks have a café on site where you can get good wholesome snacks, such as baked potatoes and pasta dishes. Most skateboarders make themselves a packed lunch to take to the park as it's a cheaper alternative.

This is the recommended intake for a balanced and healthy diet, which is essential for skateboarders.

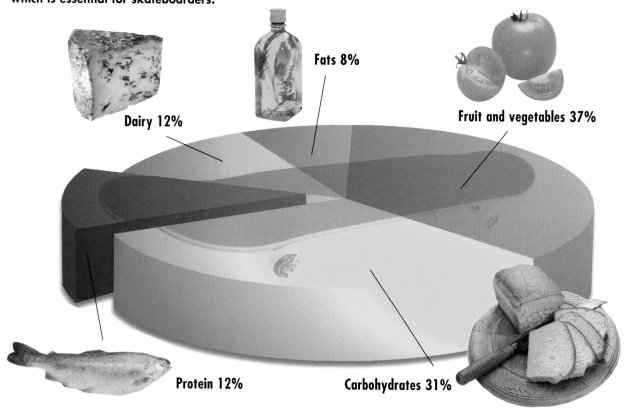

Dairy 12%

Fats 8%

Fruit and vegetables 37%

Protein 12%

Carbohydrates 31%

ENERGY BOOSTERS

Carbohydrates are great for producing energy. If you are planning a hard day's skating it would be wise to prepare yourself a big bowl of pasta to take along in your backpack. It's also a good idea to take some fruit in your lunchbox for a healthy snack later on.

Most skateboarders have a lot of things that they will need to use throughout the day.

Most of all it's important to keep hydrated with plenty of water, so keep a large bottle with you at all times.

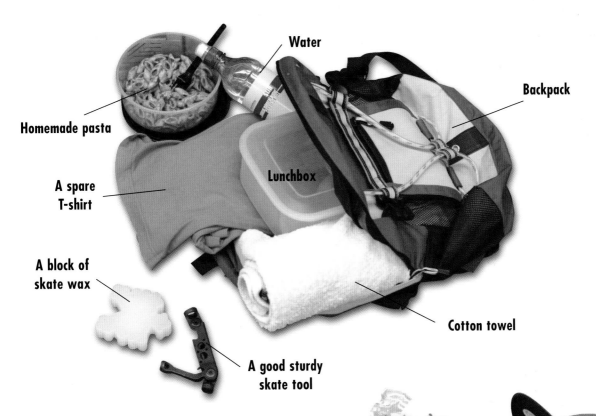

Water

Backpack

Homemade pasta

Lunchbox

A spare T-shirt

A block of skate wax

Cotton towel

A good sturdy skate tool

A must for all skateboarders is a good sturdy skatetool (see page 5). You can also take a block of wax with you to rub on rails and your trucks to make sure your slides and grinds are fast and smooth.

WATER

It's easy to become dehydrated while you're skating, especially if you're skating outside in summer, or at an indoor park.

When you sweat you lose lots of water from your body. Replace this by drinking lots of water. You can also drink sports drinks which will help to keep your salt and energy levels up.

TOP TIP
A change of T-shirt and towel is a must for a long session as you will sweat heavily when you exercise and skate.

INJURIES

As with all forms of sporting activities, skateboarding can produce a few injuries, usually to the wrists and ankles.

WRIST

If you slam your hand down too hard you could sprain your wrist.
You can avoid this by rolling to the side and falling onto your bottom.
You can buy wrist guards with a plastic shield that covers the wrist and the palm of your hand. These can help to prevent wrist sprains. Try not to skate whilst injured, it will only prolong the healing process.

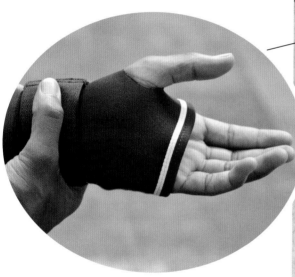

ANKLE

Ankle injuries are quite common amongst skateboarders.
If you have twisted or sprained your ankle the best thing to do is put ice on the affected area as soon as you can and also elevate the leg. You should also rest the ankle, keeping weight off it as much as possible. If you are worried you should always see your doctor.
There are many supports that will help protect your ankle from spraining while still letting you skate freely.

If you twist your ankle there are a few things that you can do.

Put ice on there as soon as you can to help the swelling go down. There are a few creams and gels that are great for speeding up the recovery of a sprained ankle.

ARNICA CREAM:

This is a natural product that helps bring the bruising out.

Rub the Arnica cream on a few times a day and you should see the bruising appear a lot faster than normal. This helps the body disperse the bruise and will have you up and skateboarding sooner.

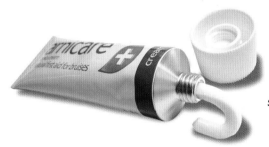

TIGER BALM:

Tiger balm is great for when you've pulled a muscle or have sore joints.

It has warming properties and will relax the muscles, letting the sprain work its way free. It has a strong medical smell and will heat up the affected area, bringing comfort and relief to the user.

TOP TIP

Skate with a group of friends, so that if you do hurt yourself you will have immediate help. If you do sprain your ankle or wrist do not continue skateboarding; it will only make it worse. Take time out and rest yourself. There's plenty of time to get gnarly...

HOW THE FAMOUS DO IT

All skateboarders skate for fun and enjoyment, but for a handful of people it can become a full-time job. Imagine earning money doing something that you love and would do for free anyway! For Tony Hawk and Geoff Rowley this has become a reality. Through hard work, skill and determination they have made a pastime into a career.

GEOFF ROWLEY

Geoff Rowley started skateboarding on the streets of Liverpool, England at the age of 13.
He quickly became noticed by the British skateboard team 'Deathbox' who sponsored him and took him to competitions all over Europe. Deathbox became 'Flip Skateboards' and moved to the USA, taking Geoff with them. Geoff soon got noticed and appeared in many US skate videos and magazines. Geoff has been a professional skateboarder for over a decade and is widely thought of as the best street skater in the world.
He appears in 'Tony Hawk's Pro Skater' game and continues to push street skating to the limit.

Geoff Rowley lipslides a kinked handrail in his new hometown of Orange County, California.

Tony Hawk showing off his signature moves for the crowd in Orange, California.

TONY HAWK

Tony Hawk is the most famous skateboarder in the world.
He has been skateboarding for over 30 years and is probably the best vert ramp skateboarder the world has ever seen. Tony invented a lot of the vert ramp tricks that you see on TV today and in 1999 landed the first ever 900 (two and a half spins in the air). Tony Hawk retired from competitive skateboarding when he reached 31, but still continues to skate, learn tricks and do demos. Tony has a rollercoaster ride named after him and has set up a charity named 'The Tony Hawk Foundation' which helps to build skateparks in poor neighbourhoods.

RISE UP THE RANKS

The journey to becoming a professional skateboarder is a long process and should not be chased.
If you are talented enough and do well in skateboarding competitions, sponsorship will come to you.

PROGRESSION OF A PRO SKATER

1. *Start skateboarding with your friends. Travel around your neighbourhood exploring the local terrain.*

2. *Enter local competitions. If you do well maybe the local skatestore will give you a deck or a T-shirt.*

3. *If you feel you are good enough, film some tricks and send the tape to your favourite skateboard company.*

4. *At this point you may start to receive monthly packages of decks, tees and wheels, etc.*

5. *Hopefully you will be entering competitions and doing well, maybe filming sections for a team video.*

6. *A small number of really good skateboarders will get their own signature shoe – and this means big money!*

7. *Travel around the world skateboarding and doing demos, and shooting photos for major skate magazines.*

8. *At the top of the professional ladder you may appear in video games and TV ads.*

TOP TIP

If you think that you are good enough to be sponsored try to enter lots of competitions, and skate at the most popular skateparks. That way other skaters will notice your skills and the word will spread. Don't be too pushy or try to show off. There's no need – just enjoy skateboarding!

GLOSSARY

BACKSIDE - *This is where your back is towards the obstacle that you are skating or facing the direction that you are carving.*

BLOCK - *A flat rectangular-shaped block with coping on the topside edges.*

CARVING - *This is where you use the transition/curve of a ramp to help you turn or carve.*

COPING - *The metal edge running along the top of a ramp or block.*

FAKIE - *Riding backwards.*

FLAT BANK - *A flat slope without a transition or curve to it (around 45°).*

FLATBAR - *A free-standing length of steel.*

FRONTSIDE - *This is where your front/chest is towards the obstacle that you are skating or facing the direction that you are carving.*

GOOFY - *Skaters who skate with the right foot forward, at the front of the deck.*

GRIND - *When the trucks grind along metal or coping.*

HALFPIPE - *This is made from two quarterpipes facing each other. There is a small section of 'flat' in* between the two quarterpipes to give you more time when moving from one to the other.

HEEL EDGE - *The edge of your deck nearest your heel.*

MINI-RAMP - *A small ramp with transitions on both sides.*

QUARTERPIPE - *This is half of a halfpipe with one transition and stands by itself in a skatepark.*

RAIL - *A metal rail found in skateparks or in public spaces.*

REGULAR - *Skaters who skate with the left foot forward, at the front of the deck.*

SHRED - *To skate fast and with confidence.*

TERRAIN - *This is anything or anywhere that you may skate, for example, a skatepark or ramp is terrain.*

TOE EDGE - *The edge of your deck nearest your toes.*

TRANSITION - *The curve at the bottom of a ramp to help you ride up the surface.*

VERT RAMP - *A large ramp with vertical walls at the top of the transitions.*

FURTHER INFORMATION

Sidewalk skateboarding magazine
Monthly skateboarding magazine that covers the UK skateboard scene and the events and competitions that happen within the United Kingdom and Europe.

Transworld skateboarding magazine
American based skateboarding magazine that covers the worldwide skateboard scene. With articles from various countries and American skateboard teams.

www.sidewalkmag.com
The UK's one stop skateboarding website. With amazing new skateboarding clips uploaded every day and a very prominent forum to discuss all your skateboarding needs.

http://skateboarding.transworld.net
American website for Transworld magazine. Plenty of news, views and new skateboarding clips.